STRATEGIC SELLING &THE HUMAN FACTOR

By M.Miegeville

About the author :

Today independent and in situation of handicap, Marc has launched :

Marc.strategy.consulting

to support tailored made training for Sales organization.
He also gives conferences / debates based on the Human factor and Strategic Selling in three languages English, French and Spanish in business schools and universities

He can be contacted @ the following mail address :

Marc.stgy.consult@gmail.com

Author Background :

Marc has held several sales management positions during over 25 years.

During those years he has worked in Southern Europe, West Africa and South East Asia in direct contact with major international companies.

Ultimately he managed during three years from France a three location commercial department (France/ Uk /Romania) preparing bids for EACR region (Europe, Africa, Caspian , Russia) for a major service company.

His academic background –French & American literature, acting , had nothing to do with the future scope of his work and assignments where he succeeded well .

During his entire career in a very technical environment his strength has always been the understanding of his customers and their needs.
The Human Factor

His ability to listen to customer and to define the right strategy was and remain his strength.

TABLE OF CONTENTS

P.10 The Human Factor

P.13 A Cabinda experience

P.18 Target- Which & Why

P.24 Strategy-Customer – How
- Customer needs
- Golden silence
- Open questions

P.38 Sherlock Holmes approach
- No stone unturned
- Information cross check
- Top down investigation

P.47 Decision Makers
- 4 types of individuals

P.51 the WIFT customer
- Decision criteria

P.57 Strategy – Competition
- The WIFT Competitors

P.61 Strategy- main factors
- Perception
- Trust
- Differentiation
- Creativity
- Solutions testing
- Fit for purpose solutions

P.86 Strategy –your Company
- Coach your experts
- Get the best of your organization

P.95 Tender &Proposal
- The 4 cases tender
- The bid response
- The secret drawers

P.116 Negotiation
- Objective zero discount
- Closing the deal

P.130 Debriefs & final words

PREFACE

The following is based on personal experience…years of work on project selling and bid management. Nothing here is pure science but at least some of it is relevant to help sales people and sales management in their activity.

This is intended to be a sales & commercial toolbox, nothing else.
The emphasis is put all along on the "Human factor "and the importance one should give to people. People first.

People within customer organization, people within his

own organization. This is why the modest recommendations given drawn from years of selling and bid management practise in the industry are, I believe, of use and applicable in most businesses with lengthy and complex project structures. Human is everywhere.

Some comments will appear like evidences or just common sense and often they are. But if reminding of those evidences help the reader win a project that he might have lost, then this will have modestly served the purpose.

In a world where algorithms are everywhere it is essential to insist on the Human factor. It is much more fun to share and work with,

to talk to, to drink and eat with, to love … and sell to People.
To minimize the importance of the Human factor in Sales is, in my opinion, pure nonsense.

THE HUMAN FACTOR

Perception-Trust-Differentiation

THE HUMAN FACTOR

Selling today has something common with the first bartering some 11.000 years ago; it happened between two human beings exchanging products, both smart enough to perceive their own interest in this new mode of transaction (the first win-win deal!)

Trust had to be established and « Human factor » had been determining.

Perception , Trust and Differentiation are sometimes irrational but they can be worked on :

Perception can be modified
Trust can be increased
Differentiation can be promoted

We should always remember it and make sure in each commercial and selling process including major businesses with complex processes that the Human Factor is most of the time determining and central above any other or, as a minimum, always one of the most important.

People is key.

« Hey Cam…, but … what are you doing here? »
Company representative Cabinda Angola.

Back quite some time ago in the enclave of Cabinda. A small province between Congo Brazzaville and Republic democratic of Congo pertaining to Angola; A very rich province with huge oil reserves exploited mainly at the time by a single US company. At that time and since more than 20 years civil war was ongoing.
Being stationed in Pointe Noire - Congo Brazzaville-I had decided to go visit this company in Cabinda as it was one of the

biggest buyer of subsea wellheads- an important market for our company- in the region.
Appointment taken, small and rather unsafe plane between Pointe Noire and Cabinda "airport".
Upon arrival impressive view of half a dozen of UN helicopters stationed there as a reminder of the civil war situation.
Immediate transfer into a big military type helicopter and flight to Company base.
Not the type of trip you would like to make for vacations.

What was I doing there?
This is exactly the feeling I had when the Company man slided the door of his huge warehouse where dozens of our competitor's subsea wellheads were laying on the

ground and shelves. I had never seen so much competitor material in my life.
The customer's rep was polite while totally surprised by my presence … I was most probably, at the time ,one of the first, if not the first , sales representative of my company to visit this extremely big remote West African potential account.
After a few hours in the base, two or three of those horrible American coffees, he sent me back to Cabinda airport.
I thought he would at least buy something from me, I tried, even small, as a reward for the effort to have travelled to this hostile location, to have endured his coffee… but it didn't happen.

This company was at the time working essentially with one of our main competitors and did not buy from us; their history, their preference, their operational habit was with other and their buying decision was mainly taken in California where our competitor had its headquarters too.

10 Years down the road our company had worked hard to secure a Frame Agreement with this customer and I had the pleasure, from our French plant, to orchestrate one of the major contract won in Kazakhstan. *Management and sales force had efficiently concurred to secure the account…*

Most of the time it is just not worth spending time and effort to go after something unrealistic.
The same goes with the selection of the projects or customer you and your team decide to target in your sales forecast.
They need to be attainable, worth the efforts for your company and part of a global strategy.

In Cabinda at the time I was just too alone and way too early…and probably not focusing on the right product either.

***

Appropriate Timing of the sales effort with fit for purpose solutions and team work with management are essential to success.

TARGET SELECTION
THE WHICH AND THE WHY

THE WHICH AND THE WHY
SELECTION OF TARGETS

Targeted projects and / or customers must be identified as early as possible to allow the necessary upfront work; a 12 to 18 months period is ideal to set up the optimum strategy. This is typically the time anyway when project become active on rolling forecast. On big sizes project it can be more. The earliest, the best!
This is the first and important step in the selling process.

When selecting the project(s) or this new customer you decide to target consideration need to be given to several factors to be carefully evaluated.

Answers to the following questions need to be formulated. You may not- and you will not- have all the answers at this stage -but a first cut thought is required on each item.

Is this customer globally or in this particular operational area an historical client of my company or not?
If he is, is it critical to maintain my leadership? How easy will it be or not?

If he is not, is this the right time to go after it?
Will this significantly increase my market-share, how much efforts and chances?

Will I have my management support? Would this move be part of a global strategy or a one "coup" shot?
Will it be profitable enough? Will it be heavily targeted by my competitor(s) – Often go together.

What chances to win it at the end of the day?
Do I have strong supporters who will potentially work on the project in this company?
Do I have blockers already identified? How influential are they?

What existing and non-existing resources will be necessary? Some business may need investing in

new operational support. Is it worth?
If they are known to require local content or technology transfer do you anticipate it to be feasible?

How is the period and the overall business looking like? During strong expansion period it might be enough to maintain business and market share with your fast growing customer accounts and only support niche markets (where you have a specific advantage on one product) on non-core customers.
In tougher times it might be necessary to go strongly after non-core or new customers to try to increase your market share, provided you have your full company support to do so.

Are my company goals aligned with this customer corporate objectives? Is the project falling in line with those?

One important thing to remember: if your management does not support your choice it is sometimes that they have information that you do not possess. After being a good advocate of your proposal, if it still does not get support, drop it.

Once the project or new customer opportunity has been identified as an interesting, attainable target, and validated as a goal by your various levels of management a specific strategy needs to defined in order to be the winner. It will be fine-tuned, in time, along the process, following three main axes.

STRATEGY / CUSTOMER ACTION PLAN

THE HOW
AXES OF STRATEGY.

Industrial projects are often a complex puzzle.
The strategy is implemented around three main axes which intermediate outcome will be the tender documents and final outcome will be the proposal and the final negotiation.

The three main axes of work are the 3 C's:

Your customer
Your competition
Your company

**1-Your customer
the Sherlock Holmes approach**

Listen to the needs, collect information , verify , assess individuals role, analyse to understand, imagine and test solutions.
By far the most important .It doesn't guarantee you the success but if you do not spend the necessary time to do it loss is guaranteed.

**2 - Your competitor(s)
You need a clear picture**

Who are they?

What are they strengths with this customer or/ and in the area?

Will they focus on this project and with which resources?

What track history do they have with this customer and with the specific people involved with the project if any?

The more you will be able to answer those items the best.

We will see that this is very often forgotten mainly by lack of knowledge of the main competitors' strengths and weaknesses.

Over the years I have noticed that most sales people have little knowledge of their competitor(s). People working for market leaders have a tendency to focus on their own forces and disregard or minimize their competitor(s) capabilities. Big mistake.

3 - Your company:
 You will never succeed alone !

Increase project awareness as soon as possible with your management to get full support acceptance

Create project awareness in advance with the plant(s) to be later involved.

Prepare the various support departments managers you will need in the organization - Commercial group, Supply chain , Finance, Engineering , Manufacturing, HSE…-
The link with the bid or commercial manager is essential as he will ultimately interface internally to support your strategic plan. Keep him always in the loop.

The more your internal supports will understand the needs and resources required, the more they will feel they are part of your strategy the best support they will provide.
In the case of active agents involved, Coach them.

UNDERSTANDING CUSTOMER NEEDS IS KEY TO YOUR SUCCESS

The key in project selling does not essentially rely on products quality price level , delivery capabilities, proof of good engineering support, supply chain efficiency, manufacturing expertise and locations, aftermarket support, agent influence, sales force motivation, reputation , financial solidity …put them in the order of your choice !

All those items are all good to have and will typically fully satisfy the ego of plant departments managers and personnel not directly confronted with customers in their daily business.

Yes they are very important.
Yet they can be useless.

…totally useless if Listening and Understanding of your customer company's needs fail or are incomplete.

…totally useless if Listening and Understanding of the motivation of *each individual* involved in the decision process has not been covered and as much as possible satisfied or neutralized in your proposal.

Solutions you will propose will ultimately also need to be "fit for purpose " and match the selection criteria to efficiently answer the needs.

LISTEN, LISTEN, LISTEN!
The golden silence

One can only understand somebody if he first listened to him.

The first thing I would recommend to any sales person visiting customer staff, at any level in the organization, would be to practise the golden silence.

In other words first *shut up and listen*.

This is particularly true for developing the strategy for a given project but can obviously be extended to any sales visit.

During the process of what is commonly called the project pre-sales period -which I would rather call the strategy definition period- numerous visits or calls with your customer organization are going to take place.
This is the time to listen and understand customer(s) needs first and then but only then, smartly, respectfully produce your business solutions to make him comfortable with your approach.

There are obviously techniques to use during customer face to face meetings or phone calls in order to get the maximum information possible.

Those are not in the scope of this work and most of them will just sound obvious to the reader but a quick overview of the main ones is always beneficial and might be of use.

EVERY MEETING / PHONE CALL WITH CUSTOMER NEEDS TO BE PREPARED

The purpose of the meeting /call needs to be very clear in your mind.

What is the ultimate goal and optimum expected result of the meeting/call. Write it down!

What is the minimum information I need to obtain or the minimum information I want to convey? Write it down!

What is the best way to get the information I need?

Open questions are preferable: write them down and *practise open questions* to avoid yes or no answers:

Better say
How do you expect us to best assist you on your project?
Than
Do you think we can be of assistance?

Better say
Can you tell me from your standpoint how we differentiate from our competition?
Than
Are we better positioned than our competition?

Establish report and trust.

Again we are dealing with individuals and human relationship is fundamental. During the life of a project you will interface with different types of persons – some of them will fit well with you others no.

Beyond the natural sympathy or not the most important will be to establish a good professional report with the person and establish a certain level of trust.

THE SHERLOCK HOLMES APPROACH WITH YOUR CUSTOMER & WITHIN ITS ORGANIZATION

1-Leave no stone unturned.

2-Have no a priori and be open minded.

3-Cross check every piece of collected information

3-Practise top down investigation and have an "helicopter view".

4-Verify customer corporate goals

LEAVE NO STONE UNTURNED – NO A PRIORI

A project organization in a company is often something wide and complex. A crime scene and investigation too.

It is also moving along time; the skeleton staff, long time before project becomes active, which might only be this one individual that is typically ignored during sales visit will evolve and grow as project is validated and progresses.

The important here is to make sure that nobody is left apart during sales visit and that consideration is given to everyone …Even to this one skeleton staff engineer who may end up being the project manager later.

Do not hesitate to visit people out of your zone of comfort

Be aware of any organizational change during the long process.

So that at every stage and whenever you are aware of the involvement of an individual in the project pay attention to him and cover that base.
Finally when the project team is mature, effective and in place Sherlock can start working.
The reason why I refer to a crime scene and Sherlock Holmes' work is that every single individual in that customer team has its

importance and you need to know her or his assignment and motivation. He or she can be the criminal.

Obviously you will concentrate, as time goes, on the one, two or three persons which might have committed the crime…In other words the ones which will be the most influencing at time of tender redaction and decision makers after bid proposal submission. Most probably one…or two.
At the beginning they are all potentially guilty and you will narrow down to understand who is or are the ones you must focus on.

No need to say that sometimes titles do not necessarily give you the key ; for example in the industry I know the project leader or manager or one of the team player might be the most influencing in terms of specifications and requirements BUT not necessarily the most important in terms of decision making . Typically the drilling or production manager might be, aside the project organization and yet be the final decision maker.

Procurement manager will be part of the decision but the degree of influence is variable .

Every company and every project within the same company might have a different organization.
In some cases even, with small structure, the decision is made at

headquarters level somewhere else and you will need to coordinate with your colleagues to get their support. Find out.

The understanding of the decision process is mandatory.
The understanding of people interaction in the customer organization is critical.

Same as a police investigator would ... pin them on the wall; each individual need to be assessed and his motivation understood.

CROSS CHECK INFORMATION

Meet, meet, meet!
Call, call, call!

The information you collect is the basis of your strategy definition and as such, ultimately, the basis of your success or not.
Do not rely on one person and one piece of information ; validate each point with different people , make sure the data collected is proven .
You may be assisted efficiently by your management

TOP DOWN INVESTIGATION

During the life of a project it is a good idea to meet with customer upper management to have a global view of the project and the real motivation and goals of your customer company.

If you cannot access to the highest level of management a visit of your own management will help to open those doors. This will give you the so called "helicopter view" which will help you building your solutions and proposal.

The people you usually deal with will always value the fact that you have personally met their big boss.

UNDERSTAND THEIR CORPORATE GOALS.

Prior to this visit, and in any case during strategy definition, you must become familiar with your customer company corporate goals. They are easily found on the net and will help you understand your customer logic.

You may identify some mutual goals between your company (environmental, ethical etc…), and your customer ones. This will need to be taken into consideration and highlighted in your final proposal .

IDENTIFY THE DECISION MAKERS

Information collected and understanding of each person role motivation and influence should allow you to identify who are the future decision makers
Remember, initially they are all suspects… they can all play a role.

Each individual needs to be covered. To simplify the approach I use to class them into one of the 4 following categories.

Feel free to add categories but keep it simple.

THE 4 CATEGORIES OF INDIVIDUALS

1 – He is a fan of your company and a strong supporter.

2- He is above the neutrality line what I would call a Neutral Plus.

3 He is below the neutrality line and is a Neutral Minus.

4 He is an anti.

Not much you can do with category 4 . You will probably not change his mind usually the result of past history; the best you can do is try to minimize his influence in the game by trying to neutralize him , carefully , with the help of category 1 and 2. If you are successful to create a good personal report with him and understand why he is like he is you may succeed to soften his position, which is good, but will never turn him into a supporter on this occasion.

Category 1 is obviously the best for you and the role he will play, best if he is one or the decision maker, is critical for you. Keep him supportive .Do not take anything granted forever.

Work on category 2 to maintain them above the neutral line and work on category 3 to at least make them neutral on this specific project.

Understand their logics. Why are they like they are? What can you do to improve the situation? How can you improve the trust level?

Once each individual has been categorized and pinned on the wall, it is critical to determine the role each of them plays in the game -decision maker - hierarchy in the decision process - advisor, blocker, passenger…-

Remember it is like a crime scene …Each individual play a role and interact with others.

THE WIFT CUSTOMER

STEP INTO YOUR CUSTOMER'S MIND
THE WIFT customer

Very often in many suppliers companies the WIFM method is employed -*What's in it for me ?-* ; this is a good tool to practise when selecting your projects.
Today i would recommend *we go for the WIFT* :

What is in it for them ? them being the main actors of your customer project team.

Step into their mind.
Ask yourself the question for each of them and their company as a whole …
Why would they prefer to work with us?

Do they have a proven and satisfactory track record with us which will influence/or not their judgment?
What benefit do we bring to the party which will make them have a preference for us?

If I was him/them would I recommend me /us? Why? etc …
What is his motivation ? professional ,personal …?

If he wants to work with me will he have a means to award the project to a company which is not the lowest bidder; Sometimes difficult under some country regulations.
If he is aware of this how is he going to structure the tender and the specifications to eliminate the

low bidders he does not want to work with? Does he need help or guidance to do so? Etc…

Make a list of all relevant questions for all the key players and go through the exercise to answer each of them. This will help you to understand the highs and lows for each participant and define corrective actions whenever needed.

DECISION CRITERIA

What are the influencing factors and decision criteria for this specific business award.

Very Market segment & customer dependent

- Installation time and overall costs (ex/Oil sector)
- Overall costs including spares consumption (ex: aeronautic)
- Delivery capabilities
- Manufacturing Local content %
- Technology transfer
- Sustainaibility / Energy savings / Hs&E

- Financing

- Origin of material
- Proven track records / In country support
- Bottom page price ….etc …etc…

You must list, prioritize and understand each of the influencing factors to support your strategy and action plan.

STRATEGY /
COMPETITOR ACTION PLAN

STEP INTO YOUR COMPETITOR (s) MIND
The WIFT...again

Same logic as for your customer

As commented earlier competitor analysis is very often weak in any organisation.
People have a tendency to think they are the best, have the best products, organizations, quality and HSE records Etc..
This is often just a big lack of knowledge of your competitor(s). Because you do not know them well -and I must admit that it is not always easy- the tendency is to believe they are « dumbs »
They are not! Think that they are as smart as you are!

To be arrogant and self-sufficient by ignorance is the worst mistake one can make.

Step into their mind.

Run the same type of exercise with your competitor(s) that you did for your customer.
If I was him/them what would I emphasize on for this project?

What are his strengths as competitor -product, solutions, Aftermarket support etc…?-
What are his weaknesses and how is he going to minimize them?
Is he the preferred one? Is he not and what strategy is he going to implement to win.
If he is not the preferred upfront will he trash the market by being

extremely aggressive on price, to what limit (Check with similar project experience globally)

Do it for each of your main competitors.
Make a list of all the relevant questions for all the key competitors and go through the exercise to answer each of them.

This will help you to understand the highs and lows for each of them and will help you determine the plan to neutralize their highs and outline their lows.

STRATEGY/ MAIN CONCEPTS

UNDERSTAND PERCEPTION. PERCEPTION IS HUMAN.

One day I heard an interesting comment from a drilling manager of a state owned company relayed at the time by our agent.
The ones who know me know that my technical knowledge has always been rather limited; I could highlight the benefits of a product but when it came to subsea drilling and actual operational knowledge I was off.
I am not a mechanical nor drilling engineer and had practised, at that time, more literature and acting than drilling or completion work.

The comment of this drilling manager took place after a

technical presentation for subsea project given by an expert.

« You know I think the one who knows and understand the most is Marc (me) » he said.

He was wrong! He was, I insist, definitely and totally wrong on the « One who knows the most » BUT his perception was what it was.

And his perception was that the one who has listened to his problems and tried to solve them was not the expert …it was me.

His perception was that the expert presentation did not make much good and his perception was that the one he would trust was me.

Trust is essential.

Obviously 25 years later I still feel a bit proud about this comment but this is not the point.

The point is that this situation helped me to understand that the human factor , the care and attention you give to an individual and his problems , be it very technical issues, is what will determine HIS PERCEPTION of you as an individual and you as a solution provider to his problem and beyond you , your company .

The problem is not solved yet but TRUST is established to move forward. I never forgot *the importance of perception* and it helped me in many situations

**DEVELOP TRUST.
TRUST IS HUMAN.**

The highest the level of trust developed between first individuals and then companies the best situation you will end up with.

Follow up on commitments is mandatory to establish trust.

Whoever you deal with there is one thing which is not negotiable:

Always do what you said you would.

Always follow up and close on an issue raised during a meeting. Give a time frame and respect it.
Same as with your children if you have.

You know it would be extremely negative not to hold your words; they would not trust you anymore and your authority would be damaged.
Same here! Each issue raised, written down and committed to needs to be addressed in a timely manner.

Be Yourself !

Empathy, sympathy, trust …will only happen if in addition of your professional attitude - preparation work and structured interview -you remain who you are. Most people perceive when someone is frank honest and receptive…Even on the phone. Don't cheat.

PROMOTE DIFFERENTIATION.

Now that you have listened and understood your customer,
Work on the plan to satisfy the needs and differentiate from competition.

There is a big synergy between what you say and promote during the pre-tender phase what you « test » with your customer (s) during the process and the final arguments you will develop in your bid response and later on during negotiation.

At time of quoting you must know which points will give you an advantage over your competition.

Which points need to be emphasised.
Some of your company strong benefits might not be the ones to put on top of the list.
They may just not correspond in this instance to what customer wishes the most.

Be flexible, open-minded and humble!
Remember the WIFT… go back to your list!
At this stage what matters is what customer thinks not what you or your management prefers or promotes.
At time of quoting you also must know your competitors' strengths for this particular project.
During months you have identified them through customer contact and

have already worked to minimize their impact.
Go back to your list of competitor's highs and lows. Remember it during the preparation of your bid.

Differentiation is a combination of emphasizing on your benefits and strengths at the same time as minimizing competitor ones and smartly pointing their weaknesses.

A lot of people when talking differentiation mainly think about their own benefits and solutions; as mentioned above this is only half of the differentiation process. People and therefore Sales people who usually have big ego have often a tendency to perceive reality only from their standpoint.

To differentiate one need to compare and this is where the weaknesses of your competitors come on line.

Drive customer to be aware of those weaknesses by himself.
Do not be arrogant. If a customer realizes by himself one of the weakness of your competitor it will be much more powerful than if you just tell him abruptly.

*Lead him to realize . Have a subtle approach. Remain positive, Establish trust.
If you overdo it, speak badly and make fun of your competitor, he will most probably be on the*

defensive and his trust level will go down. This is just normal human reaction.

The differentiation emphasis needs to happen with your customer(s) throughout the entire process from start to bid response and further down the road during negotiation.

BE CREATIVE – THINK OUT OF THE BOX

This is the time when you need to differentiate, where you need to test innovative way of solving your customer problems.
This is the time where by having a global view you can outperform competition.

I will draw this example again from my personal experience in the oilfield:
Once upon the time in Indonesia was this customer whose practise was to weld all its casing head housing -first item of a wellhead- to the casing on his platforms.

One of my predecessor and future VP of the company introduced the idea of using Cold Forging to the casing. A unique technology where we had no competition.

…This was obviously much more expensive, necessitate special tooling and dedicated personnel. This sounded upfront like a bad economical choice and a too sophisticated idea for this application.

However during years our company benefited from this great idea.

Drilling rig day rate can be high (it was at the time) and when you multiplied the rig time saving of the cold forging operation compared to welding multiplied by the number of offshore wells drilled *there was no question* that the additional cost of the cold forging was largely offset by the rig time saving cost . Cherry on the cake this was greatly enhancing safety. No more hazard from welding.

Great creativity and Global approach had been the key to success with a receptive customer organization. Customer performance had been enhanced and optimized.
If he reads those lines …Special thanks to GH. It was brilliant.

Now let me re-emphasize why people are key.
Our GH had been key in proposing the solution and our company benefited from it for years.

One day a new drilling manager was appointed in this customer organization and this one man ended the show; He decided and convinced his company to go for threaded housing on each well - no more weld – therefore no more financial and safety advantage to go for cold forging- We managed to retain the business but had to propose new competitive advantage, fit for purpose solution.

IMAGINE AND TEST SOLUTIONS
From Ideal to Possible

1-Start with the ideal world situation :
no limit, boost your creativity : everything to satisfy the customer is possible.

2-identify what is immediately doable:
Obviously not everything is achievable but the important here is to always ask yourself if non-conventional, global, "out of the box solutions" are applicable to outperform your competitor(s).

3-Verify what needs to be eventually improved:

to obtain the right mix of solutions you want.

This may imply challenging your organization

It might be in different areas: technical innovation, operational saving inducing financial gains, Aftermarket support increase , local content , technology transfer or Health Safety and Environmental enhancing .
If you think one of this idea or different approach method is good and worth the effort confront it and validate it with your team and manager.

4-Then ….*Do not hesitate to* TEST *its validity with your customer.*

Choose carefully the one person you will approach - typically a supporter – you do not want your competitor(s) to be aware.
Check how receptive he is, how helpful he can be.

This may end up being a line or a requirement in the tender which will allow you to develop the idea. It will in any case be a competitive advantage you will incorporate in your final proposal to differentiate.

National regulations do affect the tender structure and this is probably the right time to discuss this briefly.

World is not uniform and the country where the tender is being

issued is important. The form of tender might be very different from one country to another; will the results be disclosed at time of bid opening or not, will the bid opening be public or not etc …
In the above related case of the cold forging initiative the tenders were taken place in Indonesia. This is important because the tender structure had to allow the possibility of proposing this beneficial solution.
If it had not it would have been rejected at level of the state owned counterpart which needed to validate the award.

In other words it is absolutely necessary to know the rules of the game and this need to be done whether you have an agent or not to help understand in the said country.

Once again everything needs to be checked. No stone unturned.
The one thing to remember is to always dare to propose. Not a single customer will be frustrated by your good initiatives. He may not entertain them but he will always appreciate your efforts.

FIT FOR PURPOSE SOLUTIONS

The solutions you have tested along the process and that you will ultimately propose in your offer need to be fit for purpose.

For years Dassault France has been trying to sell their fighter jet "Le Rafale".
The jet is reported by some specialists to be State of the Art technology presumably outselling any other fighter jet on the market competing with his American counterpart. His price for years have also been reported to be very high exceeding any other price on the market.

Sometimes ago "Le Rafale" was competing in Brazil and India.

I do not know the secrets of the negotiations which are, especially in this field , extremely complex and politically sensitive but it was clear to me, as a candid observer , that if France had a chance it was in India not Brazil.

Why would a country with no potential enemy buy one if not the best and most expensive jet? Why would Brazil go for the high cost solution?
They didn't and bought 36 Gripen jet from Saab Sweden.

Dassault Industries from France did not have another fit for purpose solution than "Le Rafale "to propose. The technology sharing and local manufacturing criteria required in the tender were probably covered by all participants and therefore selling price of the jet and its maintenance cost over years was becoming *the determining factor.*

Digging a little bit on this issue it appears that Dassault could have competed with their Mirage 2000 Model. It was a one reactor jet competing in the same category as the Gripen.
"Le Rafale" , like the US F18 Jet is a bi –reactor providing a much more advanced technology , more expensive and of a more costly usage over the years.
Unfortunately Dassault had stopped the Mirage 2000 manufacturing and could only propose Le Rafale.

Dassault Le Rafale , like the Boeing F-18 ,was just not the fit for purpose solution in Brazil. They both lost.

India, on the other hand, did purchase recently a significant number of "Rafale ".
India has a long lasting potential conflicting situation with its neighbours and yes it probably makes sense for them to go for it

They probably heavily discussed the selling price and the local manufacturing terms BUT it was surely fit for their purpose and the deal was made possible.

Has Dassault and the French government lost considerable time and efforts in proposing their plane to Brazil and some others "safe countries "? Were they right in dropping the Mirage 2000 offering? Are they not better off proposing their "Rafale" solution only to countries "at risk "?

I don't know but I know that "Fit for purpose solutions are essential and that having a portfolio of different solutions is often an advantage provided you present the right one.

The ones selected need to be the best fit for purpose solutions answering customer needs and possibly differentiating from competition.

STRATEGY/
YOUR COMPANY

BE CAREFUL WITH EXPERTS.
Coach them well.

It's time for me to speak about my own experience and make some good friends.

During years in Pau (South West of France) I was interfacing with Elf - now Total- Technical Centre where numerous engineers were working on preliminary work for worldwide projects and suppliers' products and solutions analysis.

Many presentations by our engineers, sometimes engineering managers took place either focused on a specific project or products.

A presentation always serve a goal and this goal needs clear upfront definition.

I always tried, at that time, to relay Elf expectations and needs to the engineers presenting to obtain precise technical solutions; I must say that I have had some wonderful assistance by some of them who had taken the time and made the effort to focus during their presentation on what I had relayed. The focus was excellent and the outcome very positive.

It certainly helped in some instances I can think of to win a project down the road and outsell competition.

In some occasions too it has been a disaster. Maybe had I been unclear in the goal to achieve.

However some experts believe they know better than anybody and talk, talk without listening, worst answer non-existing questions and do not hear real ones. I cannot say we lost projects because of this because corrective actions were taken but I can ensure it did not help to win any.

Those experts, who can be internally excellent in their area, are certainly not good to be put in front of customers.

Now that I have upset some engineering people I need to admit that I have also seen during my years of sales, sales people making the same type of mistake.

How many of us in Sales have seen and sometimes accompanied this type of sales people -they usually see themselves as sales experts- reciting their solutions and products benefits to a customer who was not given a chance to explain , first ,what his expectations and needs were.

Typically, if he is polite enough he will not interrupt and will hope for the meeting to be as brief as possible so he can go back work on his project. The impolite or very busy one can be very rude. You can normally feel if your customer is bored or not interested.

Our sales person, in this occasion, might not even detect it.

The damage caused by, what I call, those " *talk-talk experts* "can be terrible. The tender to come will most probably be a Case 1… if you do not correct it.

One thing to always remember: Sales has the final call; they only invite -and only if needed - the ones they want to see in front of their customer. Not because they are smarter or better -sometimes they are - but because they are the ones to decide on the overall strategy and know customer's expectations the best.

You are the one conducting the orchestra …nobody else.

GET THE BEST OF PEOPLE WITHIN YOUR ORGANISATION

During the process... way before the tender time, increase awareness.

It is important to make sure that people in your organisation, outside of sales, are aware of your targeted project.
The earliest they know the best and the most they know about it , as it progresses and comes to final stage of tender and bid, the best : good communication with the Bid or Commercial manager is critical here but also to a certain extent Plant management, Procurement,

Engineering …others that you can think of that you might need.
Get them on board so they feel part of the team , so they can prepare to give you the necessary support when bidding and provide the needed ammunition to win.

If they have been made aware of a project since months and the reasons of why it is so important for your company, they will just not be surprised when it comes to final stage.
Not only will they be prepared to allocate resources to it but also, If they are somehow familiar with it, will they be inclined to support it

It will be somehow their project too and their motivation will be good. *This is just human.*
The same goes for your agent if you are in a case of an "active agent".

Later at time of negotiation:
The most you have motivated the team, the best support you will get at time of negotiation when it will be necessary to satisfy customer concern on engineering, supply chain manufacturing, terms of payment, legal issues, delivery time reduction, pricing improvement and gross margin erosion…

Remember :
You cannot succeed alone !

TENDER TIME & PROPOSAL

THE 4 CASES

Typically in project sales when you receive the tender documents you are in one of the four following situations:

1 - You know you stand very little chances if any

2 - You know it is going to be a fair and tough battle, issue very uncertain

3 - You know you have great chances to win.

4 - You should not lose it.

Many factors play a role here but in most cases the ranking, at that time, is the direct result, I insist, of

your pre-tender work during months.
It is the time when your ability to have listened, understood and formulated possible answers to your customer needs, when all your efforts start to pay off, or not.

Case 1: You know you are going to lose it!
Or very hardly compete -even if, though very rarely, good surprises sometimes happen-
Your competition wording and characteristics are all over the place. This customer has no or little track history with your company.

Back in Cabinda long time ago!
"Hey…what are you doing here?"

This is probably, and hopefully, a project you did not select as a viable target … If not, you are in trouble.
You will have to decide if you wish to participate or not. Many factors can influence this decision; work for future, limit your competitor margin expectation by competing, comply with regulations, etc..

Case 2: You know you have equal chances!
-As much as your identified competitors-

It might be that you have been able to raise it from case 1 .If so , Congratulations , you are half way there; An encouraging step for this project or the next coming one.

If at the contrary you were expecting a case 3 watch-out, you are in danger, time-out …something did not work either with your customer or in neutralizing your competition or both. You still have the bid to correct it.

Case 3: You know you are the preferred one and have good chances to win.
Which does not necessarily always happen.

Whether it is due to your work and team work past or present this is good news. Continue the good work.

Case 4: **You should hardly lose it**
- the tender specifications are ideal for your solutions-

Excellent. Don't be over confident nor too greedy.

Obviously Case 3 and of course 4 are the ideal situations when you are going to tender and this does not happen without efforts - sometimes it may when a customer has a strong historical track and loyalty to your company-.

Most of the time it is, again the result of you and your team hard work, consistent and well thought efforts and time spent.

Next step :

If you are in the situation of a case 4 it might be time to start working on a closer relationship with this customer; a several years frame agreement could be a good option; if it needs to go thru tendering fine.

Given the mature relation you have with this company you will have excellent chances to win it and will avoid multiple risky and repetitive tendering situations.

This may also be a chance to incorporate in the Agreement products or solutions which are usually not your core business with this customer.
Some customers are also opened to develop a form of Alliance between companies for a mutual benefit.

The best structure to be proposed heavily depend on each country regulation and each customer willingness but it is for sure worth the effort. Dare to propose. Be innovative. Push it one step further.

Sometimes Frame agreement as such are not encouraged by national regulations but this can also be challenged if clear benefits and savings are demonstrated. You and your customer can work jointly to make it happen.

What makes a project go from case 1 to case 2?

What makes a project go from case 2 –probably the majority of situation - to case 3?

What makes a project go from case 3 to case 4?

In all above cases it requires hard work, dedication, time, intelligence cleverness and again…

Listening and understanding of your customer needs in order to efficiently promote solutions and ultimately reach a "win –win situation.

YOUR BID RESPONSE

STRATEGIC APPROACH
Bid management

The bid response is the time when all the preliminary hard work comes to fruition. The tender docs have been received and you know you are in one of the 4 cases mentioned earlier.
Hopefully you have a case 3 or 4.

Make sure you read and understand each line of the tender; you need to have a thorough knowledge of it to verify opportunities and double check any trap your competition may have pushed through.

When preparing your bid response
Kick off meeting

This might not be applicable in all cases but in the industry I know well, it is critical to have a kick-off meeting, typically with the main manufacturing plant involved, to start the bidding process and review with all concerned parties the tender documents. Several meetings will obviously follow to finalize the bid but the first one is critical.
The role of your bid or commercial manage is essential; he becomes the relay of your strategy.
The KO meeting needs to happen quickly and obviously if the awareness has been maintained in

the earlier phases, it will be easier and more efficient.

The meeting will allow to assign responsibility and time frame for all departments involved , identify main issues , potential problems etc…that the bid manager will handle.

It is time for Sales again to explain why the project is important and why the team should make it happen. Motivation is important. This is most probably not the only project on the table but yours definitely need big attention.

It is also time to explain to the team your overall strategy for the project, your competitors expected strategy and the support you need from your organization.

Important: consider carefully at this stage what should be kept strategically confidential, who should be aware of what and to what extent.

You may need to challenge part of your organization to obtain what is expected ie challenging delivery times, specific sourcing, local manufacturing content, technology transfer section etc…

Do it in a professional, humble and firm manner; If you have worked in advance to motivate people and increase awareness this should run smoothly.

ANSWER EVERYTHING AND BEYOND

As a minimum all line items of the tender documents need obviously to be covered but this might not be enough to be the winner.

Go for an extra mile, time to show your creativity .In line with your strategy and the various options you have tested with your customer do not hesitate to be innovative and propose additional and global solutions that the bid manager will incorporate.

Ideally they should be in line with your customer corporate goals. This will increase the chances to have them accepted.

At this stage you should probably know what additional contribution might be considered or not.

The worst which could happen would be that the tenderer does not take into consideration your additional offering beyond the strict terms of the tender.

At best they will appreciate this contribution and value it. In any case they will never be upset by your efforts provided they show a potential benefit for their company.

If you don't try, you don't get.

THE SECRET DRAWERS STRATEGY ... if you may!

In line with the above and when authorized I would recommend to implement the "secret drawer" strategy. This is typically things that can be considered if your customer is willing to. They are not in the main offering or summary.

Drawers which can be opened! Options which can be implemented Those would be options which make your offering more competitive at the end of the day - incentive for global order of all product lines involved ,spares consignment , storage of equipment , aftermarket assistance, enhanced environmental issues-

…The list is long and will greatly depend on the type of market segment and industry.

The idea is, when allowed, to open the possibility to make your bid more competitive.
In the situation of a customer who wants your solutions and is prevented to award you directly following unfavourable public bid results he can utilize those options, open the secret drawers.

A good illustration follows in the next chapter.

BID RESULTS

As mentioned earlier each country tendering rules are often country specific.
The goal here is not to go through all the different cases.
The recommendation though is to know well the rules and what is possible or not after bid opening.
Let's not be too naïve.

A SECRET DRAWERS CASE

I remember this case on a major high value tender worth close to 20 million: the results were announced based on the summary sheet of the tender documents.

Our main competitor was way below us (10 to 12pct) and during the next following three months prior to final award his confidence that he was the winner was high. He probably "went to the beach" convinced and satisfied of his good work.
Tender was allowing options to be proposed which were not publically announced at bid opening.
What I call "the secret drawers "could be opened and the sum of

the options proposed was changing the end results.

Obviously this was made possible both because it was clearly authorized in the tender documents -a single one line that this competitor probably overlooked- and because this specific customer was at the time willing to open the drawers ...

The happy competitor of day 1 lost
We won.

Never be overconfident until the end and never give up until the end.

NEGOTIATION

NEVER DISCOUNT …until you should!

During negotiating phase if you are shortlisted and invited there is one thing to keep in mind. Your price is good and justified.

Negotiation will take place on various aspects of the bid including delivery and payment terms , local content , technology transfer ,legal terms… and we will not cover here all the aspects of the negotiation. There is however one thing for sure your customer will address: Your price.

If you work in a highly reputable company you seldom are the lowest bidder.

There are reasons for it .Gross margin expectation and profit for shareholders are not the only explanations.
Your price reflects numerous things such as ,but not limited to , the quality of your organization and workers , their social and environmental working conditions, the quality of your engineers and research department, the efficiency of your products and solutions , the professionalism of each individual in each department , the quality of your customer support etc …

One day I was discussing with a plant manager of a price reduction solicited by a customer in South West France.
This company had awarded us a considerable amount of business in

the recent past. It was the right call upon their request to do something at that time to keep the relationship to its maximum efficiency.
When I proposed a number to the plant manager he was quite in agreement but his initial comment to provoke me a bit was

"How easily you go and waste other people money!"

He was right .When Sales grant a price reduction they should be aware that somehow they give also other people -from workers to shareholders -money away.

Be prepared to defend every aspect of your bid and above all your price level which will be challenged.

You have charged what you are worth and don't need to apologize for it.

Take the time to have an helicopter view -Analyse objectively the situation.
Are in you in a rather overall friendly, neutral or hostile environment?
Is this the first time you negotiate with this customer or not? If not lessons learned from the previous round need to be closely reviewed.

Answers to those initial questions will obviously influence the way you are going to prepare for the meeting. Yes, preparation is mandatory.

You are probably here in a similar situation as the one we highlighted at time of receiving the tender documents. Remember the 4 cases

Case 1 -little chances -
Is this customer, rather willing to work with your competitor and then this negotiation could turn out to be an opportunity. Opportunity to win is minimum – we have hardly seen customer selecting companies they don't like initially. It happens …but very rarely. However this is a new chance given to you to emphasize the professionalism of your solutions, eventually reduce your competitor margin expectation, and start

working for the future with this customer.

Case 2 -fair and equal chances-
Is this customer neutral and the issue of the negotiation is a 50/50 ?...probably the case which needs your maximum attention and preparation as detailed below

Case 3 and 4 -good to excellent chances -
Is this customer highly willing to work with you and the negotiation is eventually purely a necessary exercise. Be prepared, no over-confidence, watch out and make sure it runs smoothly.

Often, not always, but often, the meeting is a one shot opportunity.

No second chance .You either win or lose and this is why the preparation is extremely important.

You need to be prepared and have reviewed with your management what you can do if you are pushed to the limit.
Especially in a case 2 situation
What effort, if any, is acceptable in terms of gross margin expectation?
Review your P&L

Time also for Sherlock Holmes to come back to the front stage.

Remember the 4 types of individual:
Try to know who will represent your customer in the negotiation and if you find out run an analysis

of each one and their potential interaction. Write it down.

Who will have the lead and who can help you the most? Who needs to be neutralized the most? Remember the WIFT ...With customer and competition

Step into their mind ...

On customer side : Work in advance, prepare answers to all the good reasons the customer will develop to make you reduce your price. Have answers ready to the points of pressure anticipated.

On competitor(s) side: for each of them review their strengths and weaknesses. Write them down.

How can you smartly reemphasize your differentiation during the meeting?
What will they try to emphasize on to highlight your potential weakness and how prepared are you to neutralize?

Analyse your positioning and deduct if you are in a very strong, strong, medium or weak position. If you are very strong or strong be prepared to hold firm, resist ,don't give up , explain , Justify… push it to the limit.

The limit is: Until you should… until you are at risk to lose everything or decide to walk away.

If you decide to give something away.
If you decide to discount your price.

1 Negotiate something in return

When you give up something always try to negotiate something to compensate your effort: payment terms, delivery schedule, option for more work, better legal terms, support or storage contract etc…
Be creative! Every situation is different! People make the difference!
You may not get anything but remember customer respect sales people who defend their proposal and their price.

2 Lump sum project discount.

Lump sum project discount or effort on a particular section of the proposal might be more advantageous to you than overall percentage.

Reducing the price of each individual items could be a problem because this new price level might be integrated in your customer database as new referenced cost. They may try to use it for placing spare parts orders later.

3 You now have a good opportunity to close the deal .

CLOSE THE DEAL.

Avoid several rounds of negotiation as much as possible.

You have accepted to negotiate an improvement on your offer or a price reduction …Ideal time to to ask for conclusion and customer commitment.

The pressure now needs to be on your customer : " what if I lose this opportunity to conclude a good deal ? "

Remember :

If you don't ask, you don't get !

NEVER GIVE UP …until you should.

Once negotiation cycle is over and customer has not yet clearly informed of his decision …
the idea here is to consider that until a final award has been announced you should not give up (even if you feel that you are not preferred) and especially if the tender was one of your forecasted target.

We have seen occasions, though very rare, of award being cancelled and/or re-routed to a different company after an LOI - Letter of intent - had been issued.

In most cases though the issuance of the LOI is a big step forward and if it is not in your favour, you are in trouble.

So the only recommendation is to fight as long as you and your management have analysed that you still stand a chance.

The recommendation is also to stop when it is time. Avoid being obnoxious. You are the one to best judge what to do.

DEBRIEFS

DEBRIEF WITH YOUR CUSTOMER.

Once you have admitted your defeat and it is clear it is important to adopt the right attitude with your customer.
Respect his decision and avoid any arrogance. This tender might be one among several to come and your attitude is important for the future.
You are already working for the next one to come!

You may and must ask for clarifications and reasons .This will help you understand and get information on your competitor advantage real or perceived as such by customer.

See we warned you earlier: you competitor(s) are not all stupid!

You may express your sadness with your customer, it's human and understandable. You came a long way and many people have spent time and efforts to finalize your proposal.

You may even question strongly the decision especially if it sounds unfair to you (sometimes developing the guilt factor may help you on next occasion) but always respectfully.

Once you have had a chance to get the full picture and reasons of the customer decision it is time to discuss with your team and draw the lessons learned.

Never skip this. It is your life insurance for the next opportunities to come.

By the way, if you have won, congrats! Remain humble and very professional in front of your customer. The hard work starts and this is only the first phase of a new story.

DEBRIEF WITHIN YOUR COMPANY.

Lessons learned.

At this stage you have therefore either won or lost and your team needs to know.

In case of Win it will be easy to explain why. Celebrate and don't forget to thank each and all involved for their contribution.

Time now to prepare for the next step: Delivering what has been committed to.
Customer deserves to get what he expects.
Hand over properly this baby to the Project Management group if implied. Highlight to them the

critical factors, the things which matter the most to your customer.

Remember, you are the one who has built the right mix of solutions and knows the best customer requirements.

In case of Loss, now that you have investigated with your client, it is important you explain to the team.

Highlight the positive, uncover the negative.

What worked and what did not work?
What part of the proposal was good and robust and what part was weak or insufficient? - Price, product offering, delivery, sales or aftermarket support, HSE,

payment terms, legal terms acceptance, agent support if any Etc...

Where have we been outsold by the winner? By then you should know- they don't ...and they need to know.

What need to be corrected for the next opportunity with this particular client and/ or immediately with others? What needs to be retained?

This phase is extremely important as it is the basis of your future success. The same as it was very important to increase awareness during the pre-tender and tender phase the same it is critical to do so at this stage.

FINAL WORDS

You have followed me through the entire project sales process from preliminary stages to final customer decision.

Congratulations and thanks if you made it to this point. We haven't covered everything but that was not the goal.

I hope I have been able to highlight the Human factor importance through the various stages and given or refreshed some good things to do.

I do think people make the difference. I hope, I am sure, you will.

Conferences- trainings, seminars.

Marc.stgy.consult@gmail.com

Modèle de format 11x17cm

www.ingramcontent.com/pod-product-compliance
Lightning Source LLC
Chambersburg PA
CBHW021419210526
45463CB00001B/446